My Conversation With Life

continue to Dream - Big

Kevin J. Brown

My Conversation With Life

Copyright © 2014 by Kevin J. Brown
Published by Klad Solutions, LLC

ISBN: 978-0-692-36710-0

Printed in USA by Create Space

Contents

Dedicated to the Creator

for

Your gifts and blessings.

And to every person and every experience

placed in my life to ensure

that I fulfill my purpose.

Acknowledgments

I truly feel that this part of the book is the most important. The people I'm about to mention have been like landmarks that I needed to come upon on this journey that we call life. I believe that without these people, I would have traveled in the wrong direction, gotten lost, or maybe even died…

First, I would like to thank God for giving me a chance to come into this world to express and embody His purpose and greatness. I thank my mother, Selma Lee Tatten Brown, for being such a strong and dedicated woman to her dream against many odds. I am grateful to my beautiful wife, Lori Brown, for seeing my hidden potential for many years. I love you. You are one of the main reasons for my success. To my two wonderful kids, Aaron and Daeja Brown, thank you for your love and support. Many people have guided me to this point: Russian McNair (mentor), the late Carol Woods (family friend, RIP), Marvin Dotson (high school and college teammate), Dr. Charles Woods (professor, mentor), Roland Brown, Louise Richardson (godmother), Sylvia Hayes, David Johnson, Dewayne Jackson, Lorene Bell, Chana Jackson (mentor), Carlton Vivians, Chasity Daniels, Natalie Givens (mentor), Janice Boger (mentor), Dr. M. Robinzine (life coach, mentor),

Tommy Branch(Book Cover designer). Thank you all so much. I would not have gotten this far without your love, help, and support. Your investment in me will continue to allow me to inspire and impact the lives of many.

Thank you DeShauna Curry and Sydney Seraile for helping me gather and organize my thoughts. Thank you so much for your patience and your time.

To Denise Powell (author), my editor and friend, for helping me get it all together. Our paths crossed just in time still to establish a lifetime of friendship. Please continue to write and empower people to envision a better future.

I would like to thank everyone whose eyes read my life story so far here in *My Conversation with Life*. May our God continue to bless you and your family, and give you the passion to look up and live.

Lastly, I would like to applaud myself, Kevin Brown for having the courage and desire to write this book. I am proud of me. Now, let us get started. Enjoy

Praise for My Conversation with Life

"Kevin Brown's *My Conversation with Life* is a riveting account of tragedy, struggle, and triumph. In this soul stirring book, Kevin converses and wrestles with mental, physical, emotional, and spiritual demons strategically placed to derail his destiny. *My Conversation with Life* is a real testament to the awesome power of faith, hope, vision, and perseverance when striving to uncover your divine purpose. This book is intended for readers who are courageous enough "to climb to the highest point" in their mind to envision a better day and triumph over adversity. This is definitely an inspiring book to read!"
—Dr. Monique Robinzine, CEO and founder, The Robinzine Group, LLC

"Despite all the adversity placed in Kevin's life God covered and protected his mind and emotions. *My Conversation with Life* is an inspiring piece of art that provides healing and comfort to children experiencing the unspeakable, and the personal experience of resilience and faith in God."
—Jillian Whatley, M.S., M.A., Nationally Certified School Psychologist-CEO/ Founder of Lissie's Voice, Inc.

"WOW!! This book is not only awesome and phenomenal but a great read.

This book inspired me to revisit the obstacles that life has thrown my way. All minor in my God's eyes. His plans will never be void or incomplete for His chosen ones. It will be as He planned despite what others plan for your life. Life can be bleak but God's promises never fail..."*My Conversation with Life*" reassured me to have Faith, Trust and Believe."
—Gloria Scott, Avid Reader

"Kevin Brown's *My Conversation with Life* is a piece of his heart and soul on paper that is sure to touch everyone who reads it. This book is so inspiring. It highlights valuable life lesson and how to use them to overcome adversity. He talks about not running away from your past, but embracing it. No matter what we go through, we can always grow and endure so much more than what we imagine."
—Kiana M. Jordan Professional Photographer/Videographer

"My Conversation with Life is the captivating story about the life of Kevin Brown. After knowing him, hearing about the trauma he endured, and reading the book, I am amazed at the man that stands before me. His story depicts the horrors of a child who was abused and neglected and how he learned to cope with being failed by the systems that ignored his cries for help. There was no social worker, counselor or psychologist to

help him learn how to cope with life. He found refuge within himself. *My Conversation with Life* tells how he did this to become a man with multiple educational degrees and a life that is full of life, rich in love, and meaningful."

—Gloria G. Leslie, Social Worker

Life in 2014

It's 2014, and I get up every morning with a smile on my face—happy to be living many of my dreams. About 20 years ago you could not have told me I would be this successful today. I look into the mirror and just stare sometimes at a man who is truly blessed. However, I had to tell myself that I deserved it over and over again until I believed it. I have come to learn that my words and beliefs are so powerful. I have been married to my beautiful wife, Lori, for 14 years. We have two wonderful kids, Aaron and Daeja. We have a nice home. I am a successful businessman, inventor, author, motivational speaker, and educator. What I have accomplished over where I came from makes me feel sometimes as if I'm in someone's movie, and I'm the star!

To become means "to grow." I have grown a lot over the years. With a Bachelor's degree in Biology/Chemistry, a Master of Science degree in Special Education, and a Specialist Certificate in Curriculum and Instruction, I certainly believe that I have enough degrees to take a chance on myself and try just about anything I put my mind to. Being named Teacher of the Year in 2011–2012 was a reflection of how fulfilling teaching is to me because I get to invest into lives that will determine our future. When I encourage people through teaching and public speaking and give them hope for a better tomorrow, it gives me joy. When you can talk a person out of ruining their life or killing themselves, you have a purpose. All of our lives should be like an open book that someone needs to read in order for them to remain alive. I love being able to give. My ability to pour myself out to others is one of my greatest assets. I'm not perfect, but I can say I won't ever stop shooting at the target of perfection. I can say that I am living the life that I choose to live. Are you?

What kind of life are you living? Negative thoughts, fear, rejection, and the pain of my past still challenge me. But I continue to improve my life through new associations and being fulfilled by the positive. Thanks to my outlook, good health, wealth, and great relationships now surround me. I live in harmony with the laws of the universe. My mind is filled with infinite wisdom, and God favors me every moment of my life. I now realize that bringing me to this point was all a part of his great plan for my life. I am so excited that you decided to read my book. We are now connected. Always remember that to get lemonade you must first cut and squeeze a lemon, among the most bitter of all fruits. By reading this book, you will taste some of my bittersweet life.

Now that you have taken a glimpse at the gist of my life right now, I'd like to give you a quick tour of my life growing up, and the lessons I've learned along the way. My beginning did not foretell the life I have now. For many this is true. Many of our beginnings may have made us feel as though there was no point of trying to do and have better. But this is never true.

Introduction

S ometimes the world embraces you with a big hug (filled with issues) that smothers and squeezes some of the life out of your existence. I was told by my mother, "What don't kill you will make you stronger." That was so hard to comprehend by the mind of a child.

There's a hidden enemy lurking in all societies throughout this planet, its name is Trauma. What is Trauma? I'm glad you asked; trauma is defined as a deeply distressing or disturbing experience. Now after reading this definition, ask yourself: *Have I ever experienced some type of trauma in my own life?* If so, did it have any effect on your current way of life?

For most of my life, I was surrounded by trauma and it continues to haunt me even today. Anyone who has experienced the unexpected death of a loved one, drug or alcohol abuse, rape or molestation, a vehicle accident, combat in a war zone, abortion, bullying, abusive relationships, being raised in a dysfunctional family, know these are all traumatic events people experience on a daily basis. I was raised in an environment that exposed me to such deprivation and unfortunate events that my very soul and my memory were repeatedly traumatized.

A most disturbing event in my youth occurred on Christmas Day 1989, when some friends and I were getting ready to go hunting. A few of us had received shotguns for gifts. While waiting, two of the young men were in the living room playing with a gun that accidently fired, a loud boom rang out. One of my friends had been shot in the head. We were all in disbelief and shock that this happened. The young man who accidently did it has never been the same. The lives of my deceased friend's family remains forever changed.

The first time I witnessed my older brother smoke crack cocaine was a very emotional and painful moment in my life. I looked up to my brother and wanted to be just like him. He was a cool ladies' man, and he was a good basketball player, too. One night all my feelings changed when I saw him and his friend behind the house with a crack pipe up to his face. This scene changed me forever, and led me to be depressed for a long time. The reality of my brother on drugs almost got the best of me. Drug abuse causes trauma for everyone involved. The dynamics of the person's relationships and family structure is weakened. In my neighborhood at that time, drug addicts and alcoholics walked the streets at night like zombies in a horror movie.

At 13, I lost one of my friends who went to swim in the Mississippi River and drowned. His body was found 45 miles down the river. I cried a lot because he was so young. Another event was when one of my childhood friend's mother, who was found dead. My friend's life was never emotionally stable after that, and he is still trying to pick up the pieces so he can move forward. I feel like I have lost a dear friend. Another traumatizing event is when one of my friends had to go to jail or prison for a long period of time. These experiences always cause stress and insurmountable trauma to the family and those who care. These young men were people that helped me get where I am today. There is a large population of people who've gone through trauma, which then manifests itself in depression, hopelessness and despair. These emotional and sometimes physical conflicts can be long-term. Often these individuals never seek treatment and thus are never fully healed. As you continue to read my story, my life, try to understand how I had to fight through insurmountable trauma and poverty to make it out alive. Both trauma and poverty jumped me and left me wounded. I was battle tested and worn, but God intervened in my life and brought healing of my mind, body and soul. That same God that I felt had forsaken me as a child has made me the man I am today.

CHAPTER 1

The Fruit You Bear

All trees, even those that produce beautiful flowers and fruit, start with humble beginnings. Trees and all things that grow out of the land must have the proper ingredients: soil, seed, light, water, and time to grow. Prepared by the Creator, the seed is supported by the soil, nourished by rain, and given energy and power by God's light over time.

I was a tree that was almost plucked away before I came to be, by my own source. My source—my mother—appeared big and mighty, and was feared by many. But although mighty and strong on the outside, she was weak from within. The roots of stability that my grandmother and grandfather implanted in her with school, church, and old-fashioned discipline were choked out as she grew up and took on weeds of stubbornness and shame. The shame she endured came about as a result of conceiving her first child too early, at the age of 15, when her roots were not yet strong. Not long after, she conceived another. By the time, I, her third seed came along, her foundation had continued to crumble and her branches started to wither as her older offspring left her for the safer and more stable shelter of my grandparents' home.

The opportunities of new possibilities for me, her third child, yet another seed, were slim. This third seed grew slowly into a fragile twig barely hanging on to my life by escaping my dim and dismal reality for higher heights, climbing to the tops of actual trees to escape the sights, sounds, and pungent odors of life in poverty on the Bayou. Even I did not know if I would make it....

In my own life, the mountains were crumbling around me. There appeared to be no light at the end of my tunnel. I would sit up at the top of the tallest trees around my house for hours each day and wonder, "Why keep trying?" "Why keep fighting to survive?" I could not have breakfast at home because we had nothing to eat. I was sent to school with an empty stomach and thoughts of suicide lurking deep within me. Dinnertime was more of the same. Instead of nourishing, delicious meals, I was filled with stories of encouragement from my mother and premonitions from her of how successful I would be in the future. She would always tell me that I was "born to achieve greatness." Looking around me, I had no visible reason to believe her. We were poor and hungry, and my heart was filled with internal tears that were too large to flow. As I endured more of the same and worse in my life, I became angry and built a mental army inside myself to retaliate against all who would come up against me in the future.

I've told you about my true academic degrees. But my first real life-earned degree was a PhD—I was poor, hungry, and determined, and I earned it while matriculating through the University of Hard Knocks in the life I had been born into. This is the type of lifetime degree you attain when you experience the pain of death from the inside out, and feel for reasons unknown at fault for many of the trials and misfortunes of yourself and your family. To escape the horror of rejection and loneliness, I'd climb to the highest point in the tree that was my escape from reality. I would close my eyes and paint a picture of my future—a brighter future than I knew as a child, using words spoken by my still small voice. My present is the result of gifts within me that others recognized, opened, and encouraged me to cultivate.

Life is about love and growth. It is an endless process of stages; a canvas waiting to be filled with the colors and images you create of your life. We are placed in this game of life to make a difference. Thinking outside of the box of your current reality creates a much wider field for storing your thoughts and dreams. If we come into and leave this world naked, how have we spent the time between our birth and death? We must allow ourselves to be used and used up in service to our Creator, which is to the world.

Life is filled with doors, which represent choices. Some doors lead to wasted time and talent, dead end streets, and hopelessness. Other doors represent hope, faith, determination, and success. All lead to our destiny. Just look in the mirror and you will see the person you're destined to truly become in life. Don't allow the challenges you face to steer you to discount your worth, put your money on someone else, or quit the game of life. Don't allow the reflection of your present to deter you from the future that awaits you.

You were prepared by the Creator for your parents to support, nurture, and usher you into the light of God, so that He can give you the time and resources to fulfill your destiny. As we journey to greatness, we will have to endure the daily ups and downs of this world. Do you have what it takes to endure the pain and stresses of poverty? Do you know how to overcome and rise above a toxic environment? Are you riddled with questions about the reason for your birth? Have you wondered or are you haunted by the inability to forgive? Have you prayed and wondered, "How much suffering do the good have to withstand?"

We need you! You are vitally important to this world! There is **GREATNESS** inside of YOU! Be the one leaf that glides through the air and safely lands in the grass. You are the key to a better world. So buckle your seatbelt and allow me to take you on the ride of a lifetime, out of a maze of tragedy and into a world of victory! You may well up with tears or smile with gladness, but I assure you that you will leave inspired. This is the story we've all been waiting for—my story. I am Kevin J. Brown.

The Box

Trapped with nowhere to go;

the walls are all around me.

My life: can't get out to live

and greatness is about to take over

the little space I have left.

Can someone please help me to escape,

my thoughts and future;

outside looking in.

I can't truly see the whole picture because I'm in the frame.

Freedom comes to visit me but never stays.

Maybe if I pray it will help;

the voice of God is like my next breath,

I have to take it to live.

My eyes open

to realize I was in a nightmare and my mind was in jail.

The light in the midst of the darkness got me out of the box.

CHAPTER 2

Roller Coaster Ride

It was the summer of 1947, and the Tatten family welcomed an 8-pound, 6-ounce baby girl, Selma Lee Tatten, into the family. She and her older brother Jack Tatten enjoyed a stable, working-class black life for that time. Selma Lee's father (my grandfather) was a foreman for the largest wood processing plant in Baton Rouge, Louisiana. Her mother was a homemaker. My grandfather was the first black man to own a car in the neighborhood. The family did very well, always had their basic needs met, and went to church every Sunday.

Fifteen years later, in 1963, Selma Lee became pregnant with her first child, my oldest sibling. As was the practice of that time, especially in the South, she was forced to marry. As Selma Lee's husband, Sam Brown, who we called "Brown," was then forced to provide for his family, although he was clearly unprepared and uninterested in having a wife and family. So he began building a cypress wood home for them to live in. Although we lived in it, the small, pieced together shelter was never completed.

Sam Brown was several years older than Selma Lee, yet

he was a young man still not ready to settle down. Hence, the pressures of marriage led him to behave inconsistently. Sam came and went, treating the dilapidated home like a hotel and leaving Selma Lee to raise their son most of the time as a single parent. Young Selma Lee soon found that she was unable to provide by herself for her older son. So she sent him to live with her parents while she returned to school with the goal of earning a high school diploma. However, Selma wound up quitting school again when she reached the 11th grade. However, she was able to find work, and lived a young single, although married woman's life, and seemed to enjoy these years—at the time, leaving her parents to protect and provide for her son.

For eight years, Selma Lee enjoyed the pleasures of the near single life. This was until she found herself pregnant again by the same inconsistent and unreliable man she had been forced to marry years before. By the summer of 1971, she gave birth to a daughter, bringing this little one into her unconventional family and bringing her into the family's partially built home, which several years of neglect had turned into a shack.

Disappointed even more with their daughter's decision making and failure to raise her firstborn, the Tattens' took their granddaughter into their home as well, for some time. Selma Lee had endured years of not being able to rely on Sam Brown, who had many other women and children living right in our neighborhood and in other areas. Before too long, she decided that her own freedom was more important than trying to make her "shotgun" marriage to him work. Selma and Sam Brown's patterns of breaking up and making up continued for many years. Sam clearly wanted his freedom as well to come and go as he chose. Ultimately, the couple agreed that parting ways was the best option for them both. Selma decided to keep the only constant thing that her husband could offer her, the last name Brown, and our shack of a home.

Free Me

All I want is to be free
You can keep my body but
Free my mind and my soul.
This life tried to entrap me
I will not be moved by my past.
I will be pushed into my future.
What a wonderful present.
Night and day, I'm blind to the truth
But GOD has given me vision
I can now see tomorrow …
Today!

CHAPTER 3

Little Sister

Just because you are raised in the same home with others does not mean you take away the same lessons, values, or experiences into life. Our life experiences are all a matter of interpretation. The relationship between my mother and her brother, my Uncle Jack Tatten, is the perfect example of a puzzling relationship. They were raised in the same home with the same parents in a beautiful home with three bedrooms and 2 1/2 bathrooms. My grandfather was a foreman, or manager, at the biggest lumberyard in Plaquemine, Louisiana. My grandmother was a homemaker who cared for the family's needs and all of the household affairs. My mother and her brother grew up in a loving home. Yet, as adults they never talked for more than 15 minutes at a time. They seemed immune to the concept of being each other's brother's or sister's keeper.

Their lives, which might have been considered a fairy tale existence growing up, turned sour quickly when my mother became pregnant with my older brother Kurt Brown when she was 15 years old. My grandparents, as many parents did in those days, forced her to marry the father. But the union was unstable. They were not even successful at providing a roof that did not leak or a home that was as stable as Selma Lee's had been when she was growing up with her own children. Early in life my mother found herself trapped in the throes of poverty and living without the basic necessities of life. I was sent to school to eat because we had little to no food daily. My mother would fill us instead with hopes and dreams of what we would be beyond what was then our present situation. We had no stove to cook on; only a hotplate with one burner, but we cooked what we could.

It always bewildered me that my Uncle Jack never reached out to help his sister. A machinist by trade and the pastor of a church, he did not even help to finish putting a bathroom into her home for her, his only sister, and his niece and nephews. He made few visits to check on us; but not ever to pray for a change in our situation. He wasn't there for us, although he lived only 50 yards away in his newly constructed Jim Walter home. And I can't recall an invitation to visit with him and his family—not even on holidays.

I recall when my Uncle Jack was building his home, as a boy I was fascinated with it and walked around it admiring even its frame. The new wood and fresh paint of my uncle's home compared to ours, was like two different worlds. To escape the reality of my present situation of dampness, extreme heat, extreme cold, and rodents, I would take pieces of the wood scraps and sniff them. I would even sleep with the pieces of wood near me to keep the smell of a new home close to me. I would pull the aroma of the new wood into my imagination of what the brand-new wood in my house would smell like in the future.

Although I didn't understand my uncle, I enjoyed talking to him when I'd see him working in his yard. He would always pinch my jaws and give me a quarter. He seemed to be very smart and rich. My mother would often tell me I reminded her of him because he was very intelligent and filled with dreams, like me. She would talk to me regularly about him and the future she saw for me. I wanted to have a home like his and a similar lifestyle. Only I decided that I would someday use what I had acquired to help people in need.

My mother once shared a story with me about my Uncle Jack that I will never forget. He fell extremely ill when they were younger. He was so sick that my grandparents did not think he would make it through the night. My mother told me that night she cried while holding him in her arms, praying to God to take years from her life to ensure that her big brother would live through the night. God answered her prayer. Ironically, he lives today and she has been gone from this world for years.

CHAPTER 4

Mistake Turned Destiny

It's February 1975. Selma Lee is preparing for a night out with friends when she starts to feel ill. She rests for a minute to let the feeling subside, but it doesn't. Before long she feels feverish and starts vomiting. Concerned, her friends bombard her with questions. Mostly, "Are you pregnant?" Convinced that their hunches are right, they all asked "By whom?" Selma adamantly replies no! Refusing to let her illness spoil their plans she finishes getting dressed and they go out to have fun. While enjoying their girls' night out, Selma's condition worsens and she is rushed to the emergency room.

After some time there, the doctors reveal to her that she is indeed pregnant—two months to be exact. She is devastated. She now finds herself a 27-year-old single mother of two, whom she hasn't been raising. She's pregnant with a third child by a man from New Orleans who had only been in town for a few days. She breaks down knowing that she can't tell her parents of the "mistake," and cries and cries and cries. Perplexed, she asks her friends what they think she should do. One of them suggests that she have an abortion "because you can't take care of three kids alone." Selma refuses to think about it. As days pass and with the pregnancy progressing toward the end of the first trimester, Selma caves to the decision to abort the baby herself.

Even though she was the product of a religious family, Selma has long since abandoned practicing her faith through prayer after her first pregnancy at 15, and because she felt disconnected from God because of the wild and carefree life she had been leading. Determined, but still unsettled by her decision to abort her unborn child, Selma had to build the courage to actually follow through. When she'd filled her courage meter, she set a mental date to give herself an abortion that Saturday. She said, "I will take a nap and when I wake up I will abort the child inside of me with this hanger." She unfolded a wire hanger that was in the house to make it straight, and sterilized it herself by taking her lighter and burning one end of it. She then placed it on a clean towel, her hands and whole body shaking with fear; a thousand negative thoughts were flying through her mind as she cried; not sure what to do next. Once her anxiety and the stress of what she was about to do overtook her and she ran out of cigarettes, she decided to lie down. Still disappointed in herself and filled with guilt about what she thinks is her only available option, she cries herself to sleep.

Selma Lee was always known to have meaningful dreams.

The dream that occurred during this nap would change the course of her life forever. In the dream, she was walking along a dark, cold, and foggy path in a cemetery. Tombstones surround her as she contemplates her purpose for being on earth. Suddenly, the ground in front of her begins to crumble and shake, and a little hand emerges from the ground. She is shocked and frightened as the hand reaches out to her and a voice starts to speak. The voice says, "Selma Lee, this is your son and you will deliver him out of your womb. He will be born to serve and please me. He will be a great and mighty man." She immediately fell to her knees and said "yes, my Lord." Startled when she awoke, she got rid of the hanger, ran to her parent's home, and told them that she was pregnant with their third grandchild: a boy named Kevin. I was born October 24, 1975 at 6:30 a.m. I weighed 8 pound, 6 ounces and was a very fun and happy baby, I was told.

Deep Inside

The top of the world is at the bottom of my soul

Life is where time ends.

I close my eyes to dreams of tomorrow,

When I awake it's always today.

I walk in and out of the room of today,

to find rest in now.

I keep my head up and think of a better world,

the timeline of problems is forever chasing me.

CHAPTER 5

Home

A home is where warmhearted individuals should dwell. A simple house can be devoid of life, leaving persons suffering because of its emptiness. At first glance, anyone could easily mistake our house for a structure that had been abandoned. Certainly, no one could live there. These general thoughts don't even come close to my thoughts of living in what you will see on the next page. The house was not fit for any family to live in. But my mom would make us thank GOD for having this roof over our heads.

The little house had been built in 1968 on two acres of land. It had one bedroom and no indoor plumbing. It was made of cypress wood and was covered by a 15-foot piece of tin for the roof. It had a front door that wouldn't lock and the back door was a big sheet of plywood. This was home. Black paper, eight bricks, and six large posts served as the siding and frame. Our stove was a hot plate, so it took a long time to cook our food when we had some to cook. Our refrigerator was an ice chest that could hold our food that needed refrigeration for a day until the ice would melt. Our air conditioning was a box fan with a loud motor. Most in the family, except me, were too big to bathe in the foot tub that served as our bathtub. Also, we had to use the bathroom in a bucket, and late at night I would have to go dig a hole and bury it. The house had no insulation. It was heated by an oil heater in the wintertime, and rats and roaches ran back and forth through the five unsecure windows and makeshift doors. These creatures ran in and out of the home at will, which belonged to Selma Lee and us, her children.

Many have asked: Why did you have live in this kind of condition? I would answer: I'm still looking for my social worker or any other agency that would have helped us. This was the best shelter we had at the time. I have concluded that it was because of Selma Lee's rebellious spirit and her insistence on continuing her on again/off again relationship with the father of her two oldest children. This ultimately led to her being exiled from her family and being left to suffer the consequences of making adult decisions as a child, because of love and her own stubbornness. Four years passed, and Selma Lee continued to live independently of her family, and well below her potential.

I remember getting sick every year from a breathing condition that I developed because of my mother's chain-smoking. Secondhand smoke would linger in the walls of the small house for days at a time, which made my immune system and lungs have to work extra hard. Every year around my birthday it never failed, I'd be sick with another bronchitis or asthmatic episode. I would have to go to the doctor, which I hated, and would be prescribed two types of medicines. One of the prescribed medicines was light pink with a sweet, yet distasteful, bubble gum smell that made me gag. The other was a deep red color with a strong taste that actually aided in healing.

I can also recall vividly the rainy days, nights, hot sticky summers, and bone-chilling cold winters. The raindrops that beat against the tin roof were God's tears for me for the life I endured, while the wind would whisper through the walls to my soul that one day things would get better. Walking across the cold and bumpy wooden floor could alert anyone of your arrival because of the loose nails that caused a weird squeaky noise. Often, I would find myself lying on that same floor, placing my eye near a crack in the wood and watching the bugs run around underneath the house.

Nights were scary. The only thing separating me from the rodents and small reptiles that ran about loosely from the outside to the inside of our shelter were pieces of plywood. I often felt that someone or something was coming for me. I would hear the rats running through and along the walls, but luckily we were never bitten by them. One night, after putting down a trap earlier in the day, I heard the loud snap as the trap went off. My mother sent me to check the trap, so I did. As I turned the corner, I saw the rat that had been caught. It was so big it was walking off with the trap on its foot like a shoe. All I could do was take off running! The summers were dreadfully uncomfortable, and so were the winters; but summer nights often ended with 100 degree heat, an invasion by mosquitoes, and feelings of grief and perpetual discomfort as we tried to get a full night's sleep.

Dinner preparation occurred in shifts, as we could only cook or heat one pot at a time on the hot plate. This was followed by bath time, which took some time because we had to heat pots of water individually to fill the foot tub to bathe. We washed our dirty clothes at the laundry mat, and dried our freshly washed clothes on the clothes line outside of the house. The smell of the Louisiana air seemed refreshing, until I got dressed. It was then that I smelled the smoke from the chimneys and cigarettes, and the urine and waste-tinged odor in the air from our outdoor plumbing, right there up against me—a constant reminder of the things we did not have at home.

Although our house was missing many things, it wasn't missing love. The love of a family—a mother for her children and her children's love for her—filled the rooms, making the exteriorly unattractive structure interiorly exquisite. I would pray to my mother's God to place guards at the doors to protect us. My mother's God answered my prayers.

My Home

Where I Live

I live where love was born.

It shelters me from all forms of danger.

The doors are the gateway to peace and the

windows of my soul.

It has endless room for love toward others.

And the floor holds me up over my enemies.

You can see where I live from a mile away;

The light from my being never fades.

I live in a human body.

CHAPTER 6

Mis-Education

In my short life leading up to kindergarten, the day that I had been looking forward to for so long had finally come: the first day of school! I had already had to wait a year to start school because of a late birthday, so I was very excited and I felt ready to go. I was ready to see the school, the playground, the cafeteria, and ready to meet my teacher! Why? Because, because I had been looking forward to this new experience. Plus, my mom had told me I would be able to eat for free and take naps, which I hadn't been able to do at home. Before I even started, just knowing this I liked school already. I went to sleep early on the first night before school started because I needed to rest for my big day.

I was so excited it was as though I didn't sleep at all. At 6 a.m. when my mom said, "Kevin, get up. It's time for school." I jumped out of bed to prepare for my big day. I brushed my teeth, as we did with baking soda and water, while waiting for a warm washcloth from the heated water in the pot on the hot plate. My mother helped me get dressed that morning. Although I didn't have any new clothes or shoes for school,

I did wear the best pair of shorts and shirt that I owned. My mom promised to get me a new pair of shoes later because the ones I had on were well worn. She also said to me, "I want you to go and make something out of yourself." I assured her I would. She then handed me a piece of bread, and we left the house for my first big day.

We didn't own a car, so one of my mother's friends dropped us off at the school. I was so grateful for the ride because what would have been a 40-minute walk became a 10-minute ride to school. As we approached the school, I saw the PLAQUEMINE ELEMENTARY SCHOOL sign, and I thought to myself, *I'm finally here.* As we walked up to the entrance with all of the other people, my heart began to race. As we entered the building, I saw a sign that read: "Kindergarten This Way," so my mother and I walked down the long, colorful hall and were greeted by many smiling faces.

One young lady stopped us and inquired "what's your name young man? We are glad to see you."

I said, "Who, me?"

"Yes," she replied.

"My name is Kevin Jeariod Brown."

She smiled and said, "You are in my class."

Large, bright, and air conditioned is what I remember most about my first classroom. I felt special. Unfamiliar with the cool air produced by an air conditioner, I was accustomed to the hot, stale air blown by the window fan at home. I was told that I would learn my ABC's and 123's ... My teacher actually told me I would learn to pronounce the alphabet, count to 100, and recite the days of the week and months of the year.

"Huh?" I exclaimed. I could not believe that numbers went to 100? I kept asking myself, *So, there are other days of the week besides Saturday?* Saturday I related most to watching cartoons. The only month that had mattered before was October—the month of my birth.

The teacher explained to me, "Kevin, every Friday there is a special guest that visits the class with gifts, and he's from ... outer space. His name is Astro."

Young, naïve and enthused, all I could say was, "Wow, will he have something for me?" "Yes, if you behave," she said smiling. All I needed to know was when do I start?

As we continued the year, I was not pushed to stay on schedule at night with going to bed and my attendance declined. When I did attend, I would rest my head on the desk with my eyes closed. Every day for an hour after lunch, we had nap time. But oftentimes, my naps surpassed the time limit and ended with the end of the school day. I never understood how someone who seemed so interested in teaching me the things I was expected to know would allow me sleep the days away. Later, I learned that she was aware of my home life and let me sleep out of compassion for me. The role of the academic institution was to provide nourishment and an environment suitable for learning. For me, the food, rest time, and comfortable atmosphere were things I missed at home. There were times when the food and milk provided were so delectable that I attempted to steal it to take it home, but I often found that my pockets were just too small. So, I partook of as much of it as possible while at school.

When I did stay awake to learn, I'd be given homework. Although I'd ask my mother and really wanted her help with the assignments I'd bring home, she would say, "I can't help you. That's new math." Those types of excuses would send me to my older sister Tasha for help. Mom would say, "She's smart. Get her to help you." One thing I did enjoy bringing home from school to my mom was the stories we learned in school. Somehow, though, she was always allowing something to upset her to the point of making her cry. Watching my mom in an almost constant state of depression often took away the joy of being in school, and it became no longer enjoyable. My focal point became helping my mom reach a place of happiness.

The first year of my formal education was nearing its end, when my teacher told me she really needed to speak with my mother. I was told that her attempts by phone and mail to contact my mother had been unsuccessful. When I reached home that day, I relayed the message to my mother and she agreed to come to the school that Friday.

Securing transportation, my mother arrived for the conference with my teacher. As we all sat in the office, my teacher said, "Kevin is a delightful student. He's polite, respectful, and personable. However, Mrs. Brown, I'm sorry to inform you that Kevin has failed to meet the required standards for kindergarten. He is unable to spell, write, count beyond 20, identify his alphabets, months of the year, or name more than three shapes. Parental consent is required to retain him, but it is my educational opinion that securing a strong foundation will better benefit Kevin academically. Otherwise, school will always pose a challenge. Please take a moment to consider your options, in order to make the best decision for your son."

With tears in her eyes, my mom turned to me. Before she could speak I yelled, "NO, MOM! NO, MOM! Don't make me start over." My mom, the teacher, and I were all in tears as my mother signed the consent to retain me in kindergarten. I was crushed. I was very depressed, and from that point in my life for a very long time, I felt like life was forever leaving me behind. I would walk with my head down and wonder why I had even been born. I wondered if I would ever catch up with life or slow down to my then reality. Slowly, I went into a state of giving up and just wanted to die...In my life I continued to be held down by shackles that confined me to my dismal reality. I did not believe in God yet, so I pleaded to the air for someone to come and save me. I would cry and scream on the inside, but no one could hear me or read the pain in my eyes. They would just pass me by on the way to their next destination. And I was just trying to face it: that I had failed.

CHAPTER 7

The Church

The trinity God, his Son, and the Holy Spirit all dwell in the church, I was told by a childhood friend. I believed they really lived in the church. I felt God didn't care about poor people and had turned his back on me. Early in my life, I was very angry at God and the church. I didn't understand how God in heaven could create me, and then send me to this hell on earth to suffer as a child. Even though my mom would always tell me I didn't have the right to be mad, because God could do with me as he pleased.

I don't recall going to church even though there were six pastors living on my street all at the same time. I should have been immersed with the presence of the trinity and the gospel, but the only image of God in my home came by way of the movie *The Ten Commandments*. My favorite part was when Moses parted the Red Sea with his rod. My mother would cry a lot after that movie, and smoke a cigarette. It would make me so sad to see her in such a low state of being, because she couldn't provide for use like she wanted. I thought that the church would help us because my uncle and two of my childhood friend's fathers were pastors. But no! They didn't, I often think about that until this day.

One day I was in our yard crying because I was still hungry and my mother told me that I couldn't have another piece of bread. I was about 7 years old. I looked up at the sky and told God I hated being born and then cursed at him. Right then, out of nowhere the sky started to darken, a bolt of lightning went across the sky and a loud thundering boom noise followed. I fell to the ground on my face, I thought I'd been struck by lightning, it made my soul pause. My heart skipped a beat and I was paralyzed for a few minutes. I got up slow and ran into the house. I told my mother what had happened and she replied "that was good for you." God was telling me to shut up, bow down and worship him with my frail small existence. "Today, you experienced God's grace over your life; he could have ended your life but he didn't," mom said.

Truth be told, I am still frightened by thunder and lightning. Lol…I came to understand that the church wasn't a place where my God lived, but where people gathered and he would be in the midst of them if we truly wanted him there. I feel that we have to start giving our testimony and responding to the great commission, which is to GO out into the world, instead of settling for staying and keeping our message for the church. So many people are giving up on their lives, the world is out of control, and we have the answer, but rather keep the solution in the building. The real church is a willing vessel that God uses to deliver his perfect love, resources, life-changing word from the bible, empowering others by motivation and hope. This church should be a person that you could go to at any time and get the spiritual nourishment you'd need to survive another day here on earth. You can't make it alone; he put us here to care for each other. We are, indeed, our brother and sister's keeper. *Love yea one another* is huge in the eyes of God. You should be able to go from person to person and hear the same good news, GOD is love! Just think, you may be the only church a person in need may ever encounter.

CHAPTER 8

My Thoughts

I am he and he is me. My life began in Plaquemine, Louisiana, and continues despite the challenges that have come. Often, people limit the life they actually seek. How many people truly live the life that God designed for us? Life has imparted to me the following understanding:

1. You must use your mind and become a prospector of the gold you have within.
2. Some days you will become weary; but if you remain consistent, the true wealth you seek, you will find inside of you.

   Hearing occurs through the ears, while sight occurs through your eyes. But listen to the words of the story with your heart.

Our external and internal world will shift, when we adjust our position mentally. Proverbs 23:7 says, "As a man thinketh in his heart, so is he." We are all handed paradigms, which are the thought processes and habits imposed upon us by our environments. For many, false messages about God, love, money, relationships, health, and education have impeded their path to greatness. Many illusions we pick up are either taught or interpreted. God is black to African-Americans and white to Caucasians. Disappointments by someone you care for is inevitable in life.

When I was growing up, it seemed to me that our family invented the word broke and we all experienced the emotions that the financial woes we endured invoked. We considered being on government assistance an acceptable lifestyle and a source of secure income that we could count on. I can recall a time when my mother sold $50 worth of food stamps to ensure that we had lights. Often, we were months behind on utility payments due, and my mother was in poor health because she neglected regular doctor visits and continued her smoking habit.

Education was at the bottom of the household priority list. My mother and oldest brother had dropped out of school in the 11th grade and my father in the eighth. Given this, consider the foundation and the values that shaped my ideals and perspectives as a little boy and young man. Was it one that encouraged success? I think not.

In life we all have a different walk, but we must overcome a lot to get where we're destined to be. We, as a people, all desire the same things: health, wealth, and love. To achieve this greatness, you must learn to forgive, give, and dream big.

My Conversation With Life

Selma Lee Tatten Brown

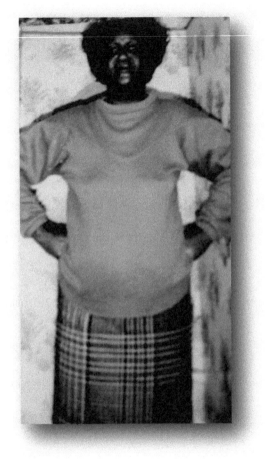

Kevin J. Brown

Failure

I didn't want to try again

Because it hurt so bad

The silence covered my wounds.

I didn't want to look back

Because of the crowd

They were laughing at me or my mistakes.

This will not be the last time we meet face to face

But I will not run.

I don't know what the rest of life would bring

But

For now I live in the present.

I will dust myself off and know

That failure will always be my enemy.

CHAPTER 9

The Gift of Hurt

It is 6 p.m., the Sunday before the start of a new school year. I laid out the clothes I had gotten for the school year—two pairs of jeans (Wrangler and Rustler), one pack of Fruit of the Loom underwear, two striped shirts, and a pair of Pro Wing tennis shoes. I felt like a superhero in those shoes. And now I looked forward to wearing them to school. At school, I could run faster and jump higher than the other kids, and when they wanted to race I beat them. My athletic triumphs over my peers were the most exciting times in my day.

The toughest part of my day was the bus ride to and from school because I was bullied by the neighborhood kids. They were mean spirited. They would throw pencils at me and thump me on my head. They developed insulting chants to taunt me. It felt like nails ripping my flesh every time I'd hear, "Little black house on a kickstand!" "He doesn't have a daddy!" "They don't have a bathroom!" "They shit in a hole on the floor!" And worst of all, "He failed kindergarten!" But they didn't stop there. They'd attack what little I did have that was new. "Look at his clothes!" "He smells like smoke!"

And I never fought back. I cried internally to the point that I broke out in cold sweats. Resentment began to set in to my heart to the point of anger. I felt as if another person was growing inside of me ... only he was a monster. I hated that the bus passed my house. My life was like a horror movie—dark, empty, cold, and void. I often asked God why I was born into this environment.

I wondered if God was angry at me. I convinced myself that all this must have been another bad dream. I was hungry, hot, and depressed, a painful experience for a child. My mother cried continuously, reliving the mistakes of her youth, and regrets that carried on into her adulthood. She smoked to calm her nerves as she considered where or how we would get our next meal. I tried to comfort her through words and actions—especially hugs. She would always tell me, "You are my chosen child, the one that will be used by and for God. Your siblings will look up to you and you will keep the family together."

In spite of my mother's positive prophesy, we would often go days without food. My mother would say that food didn't keep us alive. It's God and water, "so drink the water and thank God for one another day and go to bed." Recipients of government assistance, our electric service was interrupted regularly and we didn't have a stove or heater; therefore, gas wasn't a necessity. Despite everything, my mother would speak positive from time to time. I can still hear her say, "It will not always be this way. When you get older, you will look back and laugh at these days. You all will be successful. You will graduate from high school. You will be rich and capable of caring for your mom one day. It is not what your house looks like on the outside if on the inside it is a home filled with love. After this, you will be able to withstand problems that will cause your friends to drown. You are all leaders."

Still, the days dragged on and the routine was the same each day; I would wake up, get teased, turn into a superhero on the playground, perform as a below average to average student in class, get teased again after school, then find myself back at home to take off my school clothes and run around the house and yard barefoot; until my favorite time of the year— the holidays.

The Friday before Thanksgiving of my fourth grade year we were struggling. I knew once again we wouldn't have the traditional Thanksgiving that others enjoy. My mother encouraged us early in the day to thank God for the gift of life and family. I was perplexed. I did not understand. I asked her, "Why can't we go to our uncle, grandfather, or cousin's house for dinner?"

"We weren't invited, so we have to stay home," she said.

"They are our family too," I pled, not understanding why we were unable to enjoy Thanksgiving with the rest of our family. I wondered also if they truly understood the definition of family.

That evening, my mother shared the story of Moses in the bible with my sister Tasha and me. We learned that he led his people out of bondage. Likening herself to Moses, my mother told us that she would lead us out of poverty before her death. A knock on the door interrupted our story time. It was one of the female cafeteria workers from my school. She'd brought us food for Thanksgiving. She said that she'd taken the leftovers from school and packed it down into large yam cans with our family in mind. My sister Tasha and I helped her retrieve it from her car. The containers were filled with yams, corn bread dressing, ham, turkey, and green beans. There was enough food to last for four days. She was truly an angel, and I am forever grateful to her for her kind and fulfilling gesture.

The weeks leading up to the next holiday, Christmas, quickly passed. And the time had come for my mother and me to watch our classic movie *Rudolph the Red Nosed Reindeer*. I often compared myself to Rudolph. I was lonely, neglected, and called names, and on one Christmas Eve in my future God would say to me, "Kevin, I want you to change the lives of people with all of your might." As a child, I'd spend hours imagining the life I wanted. A life filled with Christmas gifts from the Sears catalog, the He-Man collection, a 20-inch chrome nickel- plated diamond back bike, and an Atari. I cut out the pictures of all of the gifts I wanted, and I would tell Santa to deliver them on Christmas Eve. For years, Christmas was a depressing time for me. I remember my Uncle Jack stopping by the house to drop off his usual gift to my sister and me—socks and oranges. I was grateful for the sweetness of the fruit, and in my mind the socks were like a brand-new Tonka truck.

That particular Christmas, I awoke to a gift that was wrapped with my name on the tag. I opened it, and it was a plastic bag containing 100 army men. They had five poses: lying down, on one knee, standing up, running, and fighting. I thoroughly enjoyed them!

Kevin Brown (Kindergarten)

47

CHAPTER 10

A Rare Coin

I was in my room and I heard crying and sniffling in the other room. So I went to see what was going on in the next room. It was my mother. "What's wrong, mom?" I asked as she sat on the side of the bed in tears. "I'm just tired of living like this."

"It's going to be okay, please stop crying," I said as I sat down beside her. I still remember her tightly clinched fists as the stream of tears suddenly ended. I asked, "What's in your hand?"

She replied, "A coin your grandmother gave me." Inside of her hand she held a popular Indian Head (Buffalo), a five cent coin (a nickel), introduced between 1913 and 1938; silver with the shape of a coin intermingled between a dime and nickel. She said, "Tomorrow Richard is taking me to the pawnshop to determine the coin's value."

The next day, they were off to an early start. My mother and her boyfriend got up and drove to the pawnshop. The owner of the pawnshop told them the coin was indeed worth some money. It was actually worth enough money to sustain the family for at least two years. Upon their return, my mother told me to run and tell her best friend to come over because she had something important to share with her. We all sat on the wooden porch and celebrated with barbeque and drinks until nightfall. During the celebration, I overheard a conversation between my mother and her best friend. She told her that the coin would change our lives for the better; that this was the last night we would be poor. Her best friend asked to see the coin and in their exchange the coin hit the wooden porch, bounced, then rolled between the folds of the porch. "SHIT!" my mother yelled as the cigarette she was smoking fell from her mouth. "MY COIN! MY COIN! It fell between the cracks in the porch! Get a flashlight!" We all dropped to our knees to find it. Anxious and sad, my mom cried as we continued to search for our coin, our light out of the darkness, to no avail. The only thing we didn't do was take that porch apart nail by nail. We even dug into a snake hole near the house to find it.

The remaining days of June were filled with sadness and tears. Like heavy raindrops, tears flowed on our glimmer of hope for a better tomorrow. Every day I rummaged through the cracks of that wooden porch with hopes of finding that rare coin—heads good luck, tails bad luck. Once again, tails won.

Time

Time is merely a gateway to our existence here on earth.

You will forever chase the moment of each day.

Our life is just the dash between our birth and our death.
Will your life mean enough to keep the dates
from running into each other?

Time for this, time for that,

do you use your time to change the world around you?
We are only promised 70 years give or take. That's 25,550
days...

The creator sees our life as a straight line,

Where do you think you are on his timeline?

Every day is a closer day to our end here on earth, so I want
a time out, but the clock doesn't want to stop.
Will I win this game against life?

CHAPTER 11

The Accident

My mother's boyfriend Richard Asbury had been a part of our family for four years, and he really treated us like his own kids. One particular Thursday we were talking, as we usually did, about school and sports. I have always called him my stepfather because he was more of a father to me than the man whose blood flows through my veins. He was supportive and encouraging, and wasn't afraid to show his love for us. That night he told me "because you have been doing so well in school, we—he, Tasha, and my mother—have a surprise for you. We are going to have a special family dinner catered by Popeye's tomorrow." While it may not seem like a big deal to some, it was HUGE for me because at that time my parents would have to save for months just to come up with a meal like that one. You see, my stepfather worked as a gas station attendant and earned $3.27 per hour. But despite limited formal education, he was never unemployed.

He was personable, never met a stranger, and easily accepted the responsibility of caring for this woman, my mother, and her three children, calling us his own. To his face, I called him father because instead of leaving us to struggle alone, he jumped right in with us—no excuses. After he told me this, I couldn't wait for Friday. I was happy and excited to go to school. I passed my math test and won a spelling bee that day. All I could think about was the sweet smell of the chicken, and I practically tasted the red beans and rice. I couldn't wait for 8 o'clock—the time my father would be home with dinner. My mom, Billy, Tasha, and I waited in the driveway for his arrival. Eight o'clock became 9, then 10. By 11 o'clock, we were beyond worried because he was never late. But we couldn't call to check on him because we had no phone and there were no cell phones.

Then we heard a knock on the door. We wondered, "He has a key; why is he knocking?" My mom slowly and calmly opened the door only to find a family friend—a policeman—standing there. Her heart sank, but she was able to ask, "May I help you?"

He said, "Mrs. Brown, there has been an accident. Richard has been hit by a train."

My mother dropped to the floor and screamed "NO, NO, NO! Is he dead?"

The officer hesitated, and said, "No, but he is in critical condition. They had to cut him out of the car and rushed him to Charity Hospital in New Orleans. They have the best trauma care, which he will need because of his injuries. He suffered a broken neck, fractured three discs in his back, and he has a broken arm and ribs. Mrs. Brown, God spared his life. The car was balled up like a piece of paper."

My mother and my stepdad's family rushed to New Orleans to be by his side. He was in the hospital for about two months and couldn't move. My mother and his sister had to rotate shifts to stay with him to help him, and turn him so he didn't get bed sores. His younger sister and my mother were at his bedside every step of the way.

Rehabilitation was slow and lengthy—approximately two years. Finally, my stepfather was strong enough to come home after three months. One day the doctors met with my mom to explain what my stepfather would need and have to endure to make a full recovery. They said he wouldn't be able to walk for a while, would have to wear a back brace, a cast on his arm, and a halo on his head for his broken neck. The halo would have four screws: two in the frontal lobe and two in the back of the skull to support the neck and aid in healing. They asked if my mother knew what caring for him alone would entail and if she would be able to care for him. She said yes, and my stepfather came home.

Despite being home with those that cared and loved him,

my stepfather had become sad, depressed, and angry about the accident, and what it had done to his otherwise healthy and vibrant condition. Most of the time he only wanted to lie in bed and feel sorry for himself; but my mother wouldn't let him. She would encourage him to think positive and she would work with him to do the exercises he needed to do to ensure his recovery. His favorite pastime was watching television— among the programs his favorites were wrestling, Westerns, and karate movies that we rented from the store. Bruce Lee was our favorite. My stepfather's sister also bought him a gift to entertain himself, a VCR, which became one of our favorite things.

A few months later, my stepfather's manager came to visit. She told him that she'd located a lawyer out of New Orleans to file a lawsuit against the train company that had hit him and that he would contact him soon. The lawyer eventually came to see my stepfather and assured him that he had a great case and that his firm would help him get the warranted compensation for his injuries. The lawyer said "we may have a case worth hundreds or thousands of dollars." My parents couldn't believe their ears. He told them the case would take time, but guaranteed they would receive a settlement. In the meantime, the lawyer issued monthly payments for the length of my stepfather's recovery, to assist in sustaining our household. We began to see light at the end of what had been a very dark tunnel.

With that light came a new stove, a refrigerator, and a home phone. Although, it still didn't bring plumbing or a bathroom. The financial shift didn't lead to a mental shift for the family because we were still struggling despite assistance of the monthly payment. We were ignorant to the principles of wealth or how to invest and a secure financial future. The money ran through the house like water to support the family, friends and habits. As far as the monthly payment itself, out of the $2,000 that was issued before taxes and fees to the attorney, we would actually see $800, the same amount my stepfather earned prior to his accident.

After a long period of time, the lawyer called my stepfather. "Richard, I have some good news. After going back and forth with the company's attorney's they've reached an agreement to the sum of $150,000 if you will accept it." This was before attorney fees, hospital fees and the monthly checks; we ended up with about $80,000 when it was all said and done.

My stepfather said "yes." However, after lawyer fees and repayment and hospital bills he would only see a relatively small portion of the lump sum settlement payment. Still, it would change our lifestyle some. With the remaining funds, we were able to buy a used mobile home and two new cars. He also told me and my siblings to make a list of all of things we wanted and he would purchase them for us. After thinking about it, I could only think of a mini-bike, clothes, and a new pair of sneakers. We were free financially, yet we were still enslaved mentally.

Two years later, the settlement funds were exhausted and there was no savings. I began to wonder if the place we called home made us impoverished or if it was our own mindset.

Question for Life

Is it all in my mind,

that one day I would be rich and successful?

Will being in full control of my life,

Cause me to lose focus of GOD?

Will being a leader ever be greater than being a servant?

Can that ever beat love?

Will I escape this life alive?

Can I live through everybody I come in contact with?

Then I can hide myself.

Can whoever read this answer some of these questions please?

Will life and death ever stop fighting with each other?

Am I alive or day dreaming?

Why did the creator even create mankind?

CHAPTER 12

Family Ties

A m I my brothers' and sister's keeper? Growing up I saw our immediate family as a very close-knit one built on a strong foundation, our mother. We were all we had, and the relationship between my mother and I was unlike any other. Despite her limited formal education, my mom possessed a wealth of knowledge and shared it all with me. From her I learned to sew, cook, wash, clean, plant, and maintain a garden, how to treat a woman, and to always treat people with respect.

She also shared with me the major turning point in her life. She said that it was late one night, and with tears in her eyes, she held a conversation with God. During this conversation, she asked God many questions about her current circumstance; mainly why He'd abandoned her. While waiting to hear from Him she cried herself to sleep. While sleeping, a loud sound, like a horn, awakened her and she grabbed Tasha and I close to her as the sound intensified. The room was dark, yet she saw a bright white fork on the wall, and an angel appeared in the doorway. Frightened, she began praying to God and pled with him not to take her away from her babies. She told God that she would commit to live and serve him, if he would allow her to remain on Earth and witness the graduation of her youngest child from high school. As soon as she made that commitment, the horn and bright white fork on the wall disappeared.

The following Sunday, she confessed her faith and gave her life to Christ. She was baptized the Sunday after that in a white dress. As I witnessed her baptism, I noticed that this was the first time I saw a sense of joy, peace, and happiness beaming from her. Shortly after that, she met my stepfather and later conceived and gave birth to my youngest brother.

Unable to articulate the words, her actions indicated her love for me. She was my best friend and I miss our walks to the store to purchase sewing material and the talks we shared. I miss her. The pain of her absence is as severe as the day she left me. I need her more now as a man than I did as a child. She was the centerpiece to the puzzle of my life.

The next adjoining piece to my life's puzzle was my oldest brother Kurt. My role model for much of my life, he was a talented basketball player. But he allowed the negative parts of our environment to distract him. His lack of discipline led him to drop out of school in the 11th grade, and he subsequently stayed in and out of trouble throughout his teenage years, even going to jail. His longest sentence was five years, and his absence was felt tremendously. I can remember him taking me to a game with him when I was 6 years old. His visits with Tasha and me were like holidays, although they would be short because he would have to return to our grandparents' house, which he knew as home. The struggles between him and my mother because of a lack of respect on his part for her had gotten worse over the years. I needed him earlier in life, but his troubles prevented us from spending more time together and me from learning from him; however, upon his release from jail, we continued the brotherly bond while fishing together, and I thank him for that time together.

The puzzle piece to the right of my mother is my big sister Tasha. She and I endured the hardships of our environment together. She was there to defend me when the kids teased me,

physically or verbally. When she cried, I cried, and when I cried, she beat those that were the source of my pain. She would encourage me not to allow what was being said to bother me because one day, "Your house will be very big. Just watch and we will laugh about it one day." We were determined, despite the sibling conflicts that arose.

At 6 years old, I experienced a high with my brother— attending the basketball game with him—and a low with my sister, when she tried to kill me. I truly believe that she loved me; but things for her at that time were hard, emotionally and physically, and she was wrestling with her own demons and secrets.

I think that all families will go through hardships. But it's important that families go through hardships together and that as parents your children should not have to bare aches and pains alone. Tasha and my mother had a disagreement, and my mother told her to prepare my bath water on the hot plate. Under her breath she asked, "Why do I always have to fix the water for him?" I smiled at her and she grimaced at me. Ten minutes passed and the water was ready. There was just one problem: I was already in the small tub. As I sat playing with my race car, Tasha walked in and before I could look up and try to escape, she poured the steaming water all over me. It felt like a million razor blades had being unleashed at the same time all over me. The pain was so heavy that I delayed crying. My skin turned pale and blisters formed on my chest, arm, and legs. I'm so glad I put my hand over my private area. I had to go to the doctor. I recovered with no scars. I still loved my sister. I wondered at the time why she would do that to me. The only excuse she finally gave me one day long after that was, "You were the one who just sat there."

A year later while playing in the yard at my grandparents' home, I hit Tasha with a stick and ran. She chased me for a few minutes then said, "I will get you when you least expect it."

I yelled, "You will not catch me!!"

She responded with a simple, "okay."

I didn't think any more of it; just turned and went into the house for a drink of water. When I returned to the yard, she was nowhere to be found. I began a search, poking my head around the side of the house, and BAM!!! She'd hit me with an iron pipe. I was told about getting hit in the head by my oldest brother, who was coming home at the time. When he got closer to the house he saw me lying on the ground looking like I was asleep. But when he checked me, I was still breathing. Blood, however, was coming out of the back of my head. He immediately picked me up and yelled out to my grandfather to open the door as he carried me into the house. My mom and grandfather always behaved as though they thought they were doctors. I never understood why they didn't just call an ambulance? I could have died or been considered brain dead. I was knocked out for about four to six hours.

While in my sleepy state, I found myself in a peaceful dream that I was playing in a big field on a sunny summer day. I also saw myself as a young boy in the near distance. I started to run towards the young boy. When I got to him, he smiled at me. Then I woke up in my grandfather's bed with my mother and brother at my side.

"What happened?" I asked groggily. My mom told me that Tasha hit me in the head with a pipe and that I'd been unconscious for five hours. I developed a knot on the back of my head that went away over the years.

I still loved my sister. We enjoyed visiting our grandparents' home. My grandfather was a generous man to me and her. When Tasha and I would spend the night he would tell us bedtime stories. One of his favorite stories was of the headless horseman, who took kids from their rooms never to be heard from again if they weren't quiet. I also remember the cover being extremely heavy, so much so that you slept in one position the whole night. My grandfather passed away when I was 8, but the time we spent together left lasting memories.

The year after Tasha's second attempt to hurt me, she and I were playing in front of our home. "Why" you might ask, "did I even go near her?" Because she was my sister, and in spite of everything that happened, she was always there; I never held a grudge against her and we had fun together. Plus, she was one of my few friends at that time.

On this particular day she said she wanted to make a pie and had already started making it when I came up. It smelled delicious. I wanted to taste it, but she told me "no." Hearing the word "no" only increased my desire to have a piece; so she eventually caved in to my demands. As I ate the pie, her eyes grew wider and she yelled for my mother. When my mom came out, my sister said to her, "Kevin just ate some poison!" That's right, poison. She'd put rat poison in the pie. Obviously, I didn't die; however, I was ill for several days. Yes, I still loved my sister. And as far as how she treated me, I just thought that's how siblings showed their love. I came to learn much later that her actions toward me stemmed from her being the victim of her own set of atrocities earlier in life, but that is her story.

My stepfather Richard Asbury was the piece of the puzzle also. He and I had a pleasant relationship. With the exception of the science—that I didn't have his DNA, the way he treated us defined him accurately as a father. We went to the rodeo, and fishing and crabbing off the coast. My favorite pastime with him, though, was watching television on the weekends. He was the first adult in my life to tell me "I love you," and when he told me, my eyes widened and my heart raced. It was like winning a race against your rival for the first time. I was overjoyed. He told me I was his son, not his stepson, and I am forever indebted to him.

My younger brother Roland is the last piece to my immediate familial puzzle. He was much younger than me, but we played together regularly. As the youngest sibling, he received all of the attention. He was a great little brother, though. He would follow me everywhere I'd go, wanting to be just like me. I shared with him everything I knew, whether I had learned it from someone else or through experience. I considered my little brother to be my second friend, next to my sister.

There was one puzzle piece left on the table that didn't seem to fit. I never understood GOD. My mother would talk to me about him, but I never saw or spoke to him. I remember going into the nearby woods a couple of times a week and climbing the tallest tree in hopes of meeting him; to ask the many questions I had like "How old are you?" "Where do you live?" "Where have you been?" "Can you give my family a better house?" "Can I have super powers to protect myself?" But he never showed up to meet and talk to me.

One day I was sad and depressed about my living conditions, school, and being bullied, so, as I usually did at these times, I walked to the woods with my head hanging low. I was concentrating seriously on the things I currently lacked. Friends, toys, and nourishment were among the main things. It seemed as if I was always hungry. I felt that I was carrying the weight of my world—my pain, family issues, environment, loneliness, and self-pity—on my shoulders. And I unloaded the weight of my life at the tree regularly. It was my place to escape my reality, that big, old pecan tree. There I was protected by the leaves from the rain, and it cooled me in the summertime. It also provided nourishment. The fruit from the tree became fruit for my stomach as well as fruit for my soul. It was here that I gained a renewed perspective.

This is where GOD first spoke to me. My initial response to his voice was to ignore Him, but it didn't go away. And every conversation from that first conversation was about my future. It was here that the portrait of my destiny was carefully captured and presented to me. As I sat very high in the tree, in the highest branch I could climb up on, I found myself very high above my reality. I could not even smell the reality of poverty in and around my home from up here.

It was at the top of this old pecan tree that my conversation with life began, and it would unveil the truth. From here I could see a little farther away from my own dismal life. I learned that I would be a high school graduate and that I would receive a college degree. I also learned that I would meet an intelligent and beautiful woman who loves God (and who is rich, internally and externally) with long natural hair, and pretty eyes and feet, who would complement and love me unconditionally. It was also said that she would be a great mother. Additionally, the voice revealed that I'd father two children with this woman. And that we would have a nice home—larger than the one I grew up in, and cars, many inventions, that we would travel the world, and that I would speak to people of all races and ages, ultimately changing their lives. Viewing this picture, even in my mind, made me smile and gave me hope. One day I was having a very hard time wanting to go on with my life. The voice started to talk to me and I was mad; I told the voice stop talking to me. I asked, *why do you always tell me about my future and you never comment on my past nor present?* The voice answered with a still tone, *Kevin, if you will forgive your past and present, it will forgive you. So let us continue to talk about your destiny.*

Dream Big

A lot of people walk around sleep walking,
living life and waiting to retire and die;
Sometimes I ask *do dreams come true?*
I'm so scared to close my eyes; the darkness makes my
future so blurry.
Why can't I have my cake and eat it, too? It sounds sweet.
I had so many different dreams when I was a kid,
and my surroundings and experiences stole most of them and
left me with one.
Will that one be enough to help me find the others?
Is sleep required to have big dreams?
I say so: Steve Jobs, Walt Disney, and Henry Ford are all six
feet deep, asleep.
Yet, their dreams are still alive today;
I wonder if Martin Luther King Jr. were still alive, what he
would have to say.
Everyone should have a dream; it's the bridge to a great life.

CHAPTER 13

Her Last

Throughout high school as the financial challenges we endured as a family continued, I failed ninth grade. At this point, I lost all motivation and desire to improve. I began to embrace another group of kids my age who were falling by the wayside, too. This group of friends and I named ourselves and became known as the Over the Bayou Boys (OTBB). We all lived on one of the six streets in our immediate area: Bell, George, Nicholas, West Street, Homestead Drive, and Cabbage Town. The future for all of us seemed dismal because we all had limited resources. Trouble seemed to be our primary option, given our conditions. And we stuck together. We would fight with other youth from different parts of town, steal, serve as corner pharmaceutical representatives, and just enjoy hanging with one another.

Although we were all filled with potential, not all members of the crew now have a story of success to share. Some have become addicts to the poisons we once distributed. Others are or were members of the American penal system. Most have succumbed to the perils of that lifestyle. But they were a band of brothers for me who taught me how to protect myself, and who even fed, clothed, and supported me.

Even though I had OTBB, fortunately, basketball was my main outlet. It was basketball that kept me from being a participant in many of the activities that transpired that led to many in the "OTBB Crew's" demise. I excelled as the shooting guard on our team. I can recall the crowd's response to the slams and points I scored during the high school games. To be so successful at basketball made me feel like a big man on campus. It gave me the greatest joy to play when the entire OTBB Crew came to the games to support me. As an athlete I learned discipline and the importance of teamwork. Most important, it also protected me from the negative elements within my environment. My coach would also ensure that I remained trouble- free by keeping me at school during home game nights. However, despite my athletic ability, I failed to apply myself academically. I found myself at the end of ninth grade, and needing a half of a geometry credit that I did not earn that year, and I did not go to summer school. I just cruised on through ninth grade again, and somehow did enough to get by in 10th, 11th, and 12th grades to be able to eventually earn a high school diploma. By the time I graduated, my grade point average (GPA) was only 1.9. This made my collegiate options minimal.

The summer after graduating from high school, I was still living at home and was not enrolled in anyone's college. I'd tried to escape my environment on numerous occasions when my friends were preparing to return to school.

Initially, I had decided I was going to Grambling University. A friend offered me a ride with him and his dad the following day, a Saturday. I went to bed early that Friday after my mother prepared a lunch, I packed my bags and set my alarm. And 5:30 a.m. couldn't come quickly enough. I awoke to the blaring sound from my alarm clock. I dressed and prepared for my trip, and with two bags in hand, I went outside to wait for my friend and his father. An hour passed and they hadn't come. Five hours passed and I decided to page him, but I never received a response. After I started paging him, my mother came out to sit with me. After a while, she said "he's not coming, son." Tears began to flow from my eyes and I told her "they are going to come. They are just going to leave late." Tears began to stream down her face, yet she was able to still speak life to me. "You will get to go one day, son. Don't give up," she said as she helped me bring my bags back into the house.

Now that my college dream was pulled back from me, I sought out employment. I secured a position at a chemical plant in Baton Rouge; and, at times, I was employed as a pharmaceutical rep for the block. This was something I saw

75

as a temporary job and not a career because I knew I had to pursue my collegiate dreams. My pharmaceutical co-workers would laugh at me and say, "Whatever opportunity you had has come and gone." I'd laugh back at them because in spite of my circumstances I could still see the portrait of "elevation above it all that I remembered from sitting high up in that pecan tree" as this memory flashed through my mind. I could still see myself attending and graduating from college and becoming a collegiate basketball player. No one around me could comprehend the level of my dreams and my refusal to return to the everyday mundane life that we had lived growing up.

As time passed, my mother said that she was beginning to see a dimming of the light in my eyes. She said she could see my dreams starting to fade from my imagination. She started to tell me regularly "You will be successful. You just watch and see, son. God is going to put your life on display for everyone to see. I promise you."

Eventually, her promise began to ring true. Returning home from the market, my mother told me she had seen my high school teammate's mother. My mother said that the guy's mom told her that her son was home from college for the summer, and that he would be returning to Alabama on Saturday to play basketball. She also said that I should give her a call if I'd like to ride back with them."

"Are you serious?!?" I screamed.

"As a heart attack," my mom replied.

It had been two years since my old classmate Ted Williams and I had last spoken. After graduation, he got accepted and attended a junior college in Alabama and was eventually recruited by a small Historical Black College/University (HBCU) in Birmingham called Miles College. Thinking to myself, *I have nothing to lose*; I picked up the phone book, retrieved their phone number, and called him.

Ted answered and said "What's up, Mean" That was a nickname that he had acquired during high school. "Are you in school?"

"No, I'm just working," I replied

"Are you still interested in attending college? Ever considered moving to Alabama? You interested in going back with me? I'm sure you would make the team," he blurted out almost all at once.

"Sure!" I said, excited beyond belief.

"Be ready Saturday morning at 6," he told me.

"What do I need for the trip?" I asked.

"Just bring money to put toward a tank of gas to get us there and enough money to hold you over for a few days. You need to determine whether or not you will like it. If it doesn't work out, I will help you get back home on the bus."

I responded, "Deal!"

I was a bit apprehensive, though, because I'd had a similar conversation previously and I was left in tears. However, my mother was excited when I gave her the news. She began planning how to secure enough money for the trip because I wasn't scheduled to get paid until the following Friday. Everyone I'd reached out to for a loan was unable to assist me at the time, and five days had passed since my conversation with my classmate. By the time I got in from work Ted had called and left a message requesting a return call. My heart sank and I said to myself, *Oh boy, here it goes. He's going to tell me I can't ride.* Still, I called him and with each ring of the phone my heartbeat increased. Finally, he answered.

He said, "What's up Mean? I wanted to know if you would be able to leave tomorrow, instead of Saturday. I want to get back earlier to get settled."

"I'm not sure. I don't have the money yet."

"Call me back and let me know. You will get the money."

"I hope so."

My mom was waiting nearby, so I told her about the conversation. Her response was, "Give me a few minutes," as she grabbed the phone to call her best friend. I listened quietly as she explained the situation.

Her best friend, Ms. Betty Lou Jones, thought about it for a few minutes and said, "Selma Lee, I have $75 you can borrow. Will that help?"

"Yes!" she screamed and thanked her profusely.

In this moment, I realized that the fulfillment of my collegiate dreams was just around the corner. With the clothes on my back, $75, and one bag, I departed the life that I had known with my mother, brother, and sister. And surprisingly to me, I was in tears.

"I'll be back soon," I said.

My mother responded, "I will be praying for you, son. Promise me you will make something out of your life."

I said, "I will make you proud of me. I will take care of you and my brothers and sister one day."

As we drove away to begin our journey to Alabama, so many different emotions began to rush across my mind and body. My heart was beating so fast, and I asked myself if I would ever really come back home. The main thing I asked myself was, *Will I make it?* My mother, sister, and little brother with tears streaming down their faces, stood in the middle of the road waving good-bye. With my eyes full, too, I waved back but with a numb feeling of unbelief that I was finally about to go for it. I was about to pursue my many dreams! When I got to Alabama, I was very excited but homesick and scared. It was so different than Plaquemine. I want to thank Mean again for showing a whole new world outside of Louisiana. OK, the next day it was try outs and Mean told me that it wouldn't be easy to make the team; but why not try anyway, I had nothing to lose. Now I want you to ponder and infer on what you think happen next in my chronicle life story. Hint: more drama, ups and downs and I had an encounter with God in my room during one of my college years. I have never been the same. **Part 2: My Encounter with GOD...**

I Can Do This

As the door closes,
I turn the knob and open it
I can do this.
When I feel like I can't move,
My feet take another step
I can do this.
As my mind races and I can't sleep
Peace comes over me
And finally I cross the finish line of sleep
I can do this.
You must finish the race no matter what
I can't let time and the grave beat me
I can do this.
Now my inner vision allows me to see
What my eyes kept blind to me
I can live beyond where I am now
Really, I can!

CHAPTER 14

Whispers to the Soul

The Creator did not make a mistake in allowing your creation. Of three hundred million sperm cells, you were chosen to live on purpose. That purpose is to impact mankind. There is a lot of work to be done, so lift your head, and take that second wind. These words have prevented me from abandoning the dreams of my youth; the life prepared for me, and destroyed the spirits of anger with God that were within me. They saved my life forever. There is GREATNESS inside of you!

Life is filled with experiences. These experiences come to us in the form of failures, obstacles, heartache, pain, and setbacks. Instead of depending on others, you should first tap into self. Be your own motivator/cheerleader. Be reflective, yet never allow self-pity and condemnation to consume you. Life is about growth and development of your mind, body, and spirit; however, it requires regular conversations with God and with yourself in solitude to ultimately propel you to your destiny. You must repeat these words to yourself daily, or as regularly as possible:

1. I am unique. I am the chosen one. I am intelligent.
2. I am wise. I am healthy. I am wealthy.
3. My relationships are well.
4. I am creative. I can change. I am love.
5. My money will work for me.
6. My aspirations will all come to fruition.
7. This is the beginning of a better life for me.
8. I can do this.
9. I am a leader.
10. I will not stop trying.
11. I will always forgive.
12. I will give to those in need.
13. A positive attitude makes for a better journey.
14. There is good in everyone.
15. I am responsible for my actions.
16. I have favor.
17. I will look up and live each day.
18. I will leave this world better than when I arrived.

Questions to Consider and Discuss

1. What conversations do you need to have with yourself or others that you need to settle a disagreement with regarding your life?
2. What are three things that you feel have allowed you to hold on to hurt?
3. What is the one thing that has held you back from reaching your highest potential?
4. How would you define fear? Why?
5. Do you have a plan to address dysfunction in your family?
6. How would you relate failure to destiny? And greatness?
7. At what point in the storyline did you see yourself?
8. What was the most relevant occurrence in the book to you?
9. What is the significance of the title to you?
10. Overall, what can you take away from this story?

Kevin J. Brown

Notes

Reference Page

Printed by Create Space, an Amazon.com Company
Create Space, Charleston SC

Printed by Create Space, an Amazon.com Company
Available from Amazon.com and other retail outlets
Available from Amazon.com and other online stores
Available from Amazon.com and other book stores
Available from Amazon.com, CreateSpace.com, and other
retail outlets
A reference to an Amazon review
Available on Kindle and other devices
Available on Kindle and other retail outlets
Available on Kindle and other book stores
Available on Kindle and online stores

Contact Information

Klad Solutions, LLC

P.O. Box 1115

Conyers GA 30012

Face book Page: Facebook.com/Kb Speaks

Website: www.KBBrownSpeaks.com

Email address: kbbrownspeaks@gmail.com